A HOLIDAY BOOK

Fourth of July

BY CHARLES P. GRAVES

ILLUSTRATED BY KEN WAGNER

GARRARD PUBLISHING COMPANY
CHAMPAIGN, ILLINOIS

For Teeny and Hal

Holiday Books are edited under
the educational supervision of

Charles E. Johnson, Ed.D.
Associate Professor of Education
University of Illinois

Published in Champaign, Illinois by Garrard Publishing Company
Manufactured in the United States of America
Library of Congress Catalog Card Number: 63-13625

Contents

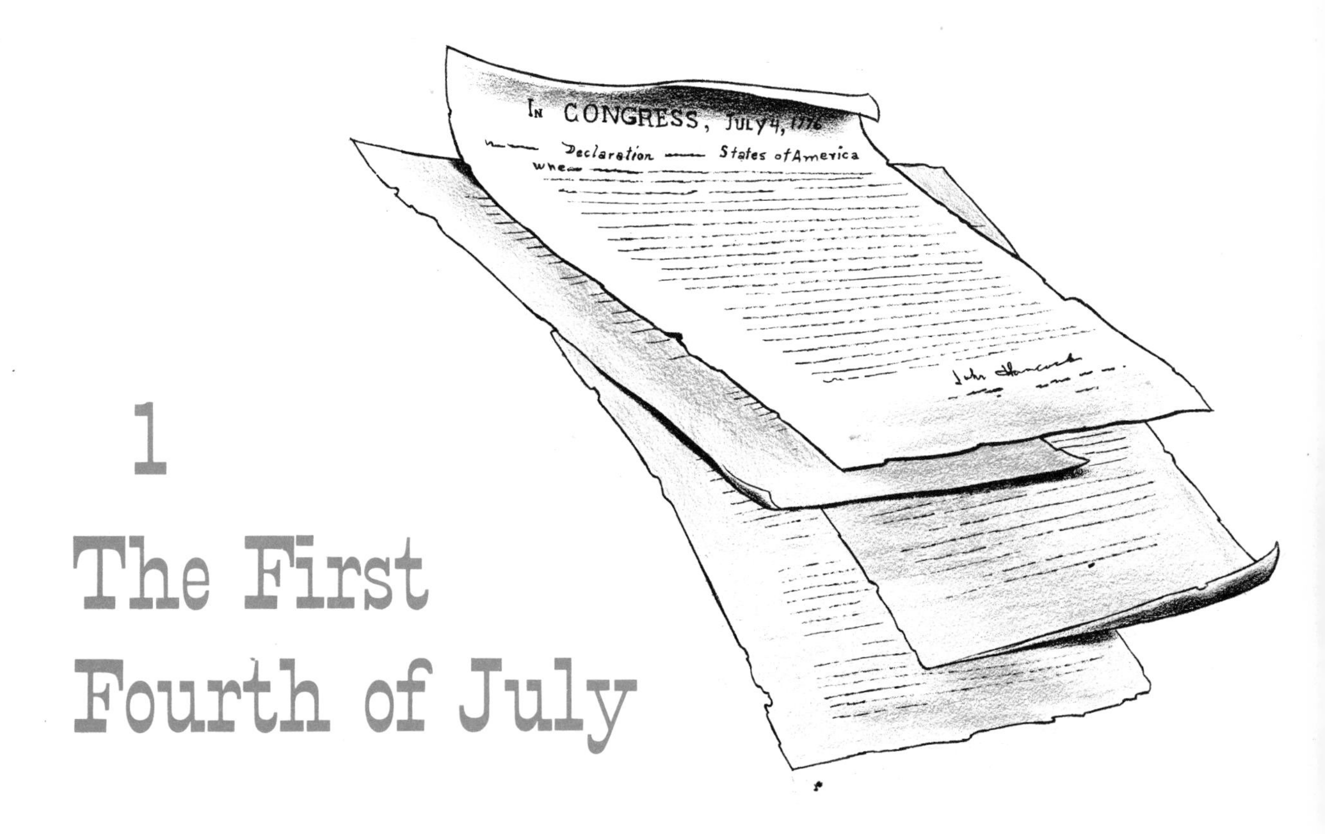

1 The First Fourth of July

"Clang! Clang! Clang!" The music of the great bell floated over Philadelphia. It was calling the people to the State House yard. There they would hear a man read the Declaration of Independence.

Until 1776, the American colonies had been ruled by England. Now the Americans had decided to rule themselves. They would build a new nation.

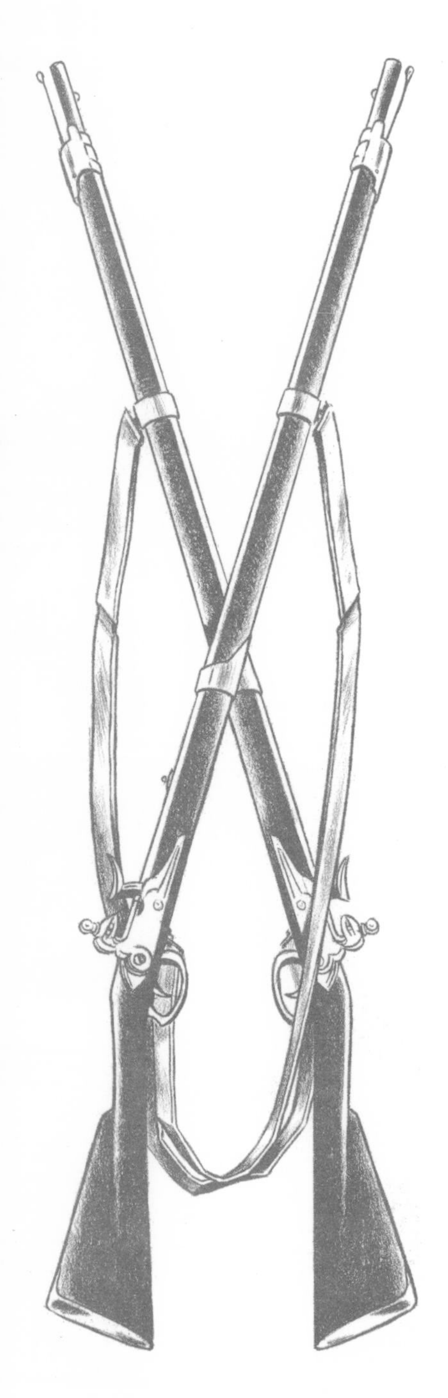

It was a brave thing for the Americans to do. For they knew it meant a long war with England. England had a big army and navy.

When the people in Philadelphia heard the bell, they poured into the streets. They raced toward the State House. Most of them knew that Congress had voted for the Declaration on July 4. This was their first chance to hear someone read it.

As soon as the crowd gathered, the bell stopped ringing. A man stood up. He read the Declaration of Independence just as Thomas Jefferson had written it. Jefferson was a leader from Virginia.

The Declaration of Independence told the world why America wanted to be free. It told of the many unfair things England's King, George III, had done. And it said that the colonies were now independent.

"Hurrah!" the crowd shouted. Up in the State House tower a man rang the bell again. He thought of the words written on it.

"Proclaim liberty throughout all the land, unto all the inhabitants thereof."

These wonderful words are from the Bible. The bell they are written on is now called the Liberty Bell. The State House is now Independence Hall.

News of the Declaration of Independence spread slowly throughout America. It went by men on horseback and by boat. There were no telephones or radios then.

General George Washington was in New York City. A copy of the Declaration was sent to him. He had it read to his soldiers.

The American soldiers had already been fighting the English. They had been fighting for their rights. Now they had something greater to fight for—freedom!

The soldiers knew this meant a hard fight. They felt sure they could win. We call the war they fought the Revolutionary War.

There was a big statue of King George III in New York. It was made of lead. Some of the American soldiers pulled the statue down. They cut off the statue's head. The lead from King George's statue was made into bullets. The Americans fired the bullets at the King's soldiers.

In many other towns people pulled down royal statues. Sometimes they tied ropes around the necks of the statues. Then they pulled the statues through the streets.

When news of the Declaration reached Boston, the people went wild with joy. American soldiers fired their cannon in honor of the thirteen American states. "Boom! Boom! Boom!" roared the cannon, thirteen times in all.

Bells rang. Drums beat. The people pulled down all signs that said George III was their king. They made a big bonfire out of the signs. They danced around it happily.

News of America's independence spread to all the states. Finally a copy of the Declaration reached a little settlement in

South Carolina. Not many people there could read.

But a nine-year-old boy, Andrew Jackson, had learned to read in school. The grown-ups met at a farmhouse. The boy stood up and read the Declaration.

The grownups clapped when they heard the boy say *"all men are created equal."* They cheered when he read that everyone has a right to *"life, liberty and the pursuit of happiness."*

The United States was born on July 4, 1776. America's birthday is her biggest holiday.

2
Early Independence Days

John Adams was one of the most important American leaders. He had worked hard to make the other leaders vote for independence.

Adams said that the day Congress voted for independence should be celebrated forever. He believed America's birthday should be marked with parades, shows, games, sports, guns, bells and bonfires.

Americans had to fight a long war with England to get their independence. But even during the war they found time to celebrate the Fourth of July. The people built bonfires, shot guns and rang bells.

After America won the war, the Fourth of July celebrations became much bigger. In most towns and villages tables were set up in the public squares. All the people from each town had a picnic together. The men who had fought in the war against England were special guests.

There were exciting games for children. Sometimes there were potato races and watermelon-eating contests. One of the funniest sights was the contest where children tried to catch a greased pig!

Often a boy read the Declaration of Independence to the grownups. It was an honor to be chosen to read it.

Sometimes a girl read a poem. There was a good one that went:

"Squeak the fife and beat the drum
Independence Day has come."

There were long speeches. Most speakers bragged about America. They might say:

"The American Eagle! May she stick her beak in the North Pole. May she fan the Atlantic and the Pacific oceans with her wings. And may she switch her tail feathers over the tip of South America."

These men liked to hear themselves talk. No one really took them seriously.

The years went by. On July 4, 1826, America would be 50 years old!

Both John Adams and Thomas Jefferson were still alive. They had both helped make independence possible. Adams had worked for it. Jefferson had written the famous Declaration.

Adams had been the second President of the United States. Jefferson had been the third President.

Now, on July 3, 1826, both men were sick. In Virginia, Jefferson lay dying. He was 83 years old. He hoped he could stay alive until the Fourth of July.

There was a clock in his room. He tried to watch the hands creep toward midnight. It was hard, for Jefferson could not see well.

A friend stood by his bed. "Is it the Fourth yet?" Jefferson asked.

"Not yet," his friend said.

The hands of the clock moved slowly on. Again Jefferson asked, "Is this the Fourth?"

"Yes," his friend answered.

"Ah!" Jefferson said happily. The old man went to sleep. He died shortly after noon on the Fourth.

In Massachusetts, Adams was dying too. He was 91. His son, John Quincy Adams, was now President of the United States.

A few days earlier a man had come to see Adams. He asked the old man to make up a toast. The toast would be given at a party on the fiftieth Fourth of July.

"Independence forever!" Adams said proudly.

On the afternoon of the Fourth, Adams was very sick. He did not know that

Jefferson was already dead. The last words Adams spoke were, "Jefferson still lives." But he was wrong.

Shortly after dark, loud shouts came from the village. The people were cheering for Adams' toast, "Independence forever!"

Before the cheers faded Adams was dead.

Jefferson and Adams died on the day they helped make famous. Without these two patriots there might not have been a Fourth of July to celebrate.

3

Patriotic Music

There has always been music on the Fourth of July. Our oldest patriotic song is *Yankee Doodle*. It is even older than the Declaration of Independence.

Before the Revolutionary War there were many English soldiers in America. They wore fine uniforms and knew how to keep in step while marching.

The American soldiers were too poor to buy uniforms. Some of them wore long coats. Some wore short coats. Some wore no coats at all. The English laughed at the American soldiers.

As a joke the English made up a song about the American soldiers. They called it *Yankee Doodle.*

Here are some of the words:

"And there they'd fife away like fun
And play on cornstock fiddles,
And some had ribbons red as blood
All wound around their middles.
Yankee Doodle keep it up,
Yankee Doodle dandy,
Mind the music and the step
And with the girls be handy."

When the Revolution started, some of the English soldiers marched out of Boston. They were going to fight the Americans at

nearby Lexington and Concord. The English band played *Yankee Doodle* to make fun of the Americans.

The Americans were not afraid of the English. What difference did fine uniforms make?

At Concord the Americans beat the English. The English ran. This time the Americans laughed!

The Americans started singing *Yankee Doodle*. They chased the English back to Boston to the tune of their own song. From that day on, *Yankee Doodle* was an American song. The Americans had captured the song from the English.

The last battle in the Revolutionary War was fought at Yorktown, Virginia. The Americans won it. When the battle was over, the American bands played. One of the tunes was *Yankee Doodle*.

It's no wonder we play *Yankee Doodle* in our Fourth of July parades today.

Another song that is always played is *The Star-Spangled Banner.* The words to this song were written during the War of 1812. That was another war America had with the English.

One day some English warships attacked the Americans at Fort McHenry at Baltimore, Maryland. An American named Francis Scott Key watched the battle from a boat nearby.

He saw the English warships fire many shells and rockets at Fort McHenry. While he watched, the American flag continued to fly over the fort. This meant the Americans still held it.

After dark he could no longer see the flag. All night long rockets burst above the fort. Sometimes Key could see the flag in

the bright red glare. He prayed that the Americans could hold the fort through the night.

As the sun started to come up, Key wrote the first words of a song on an envelope.

"Oh, say can you see by the dawn's early light,
What so proudly we hailed at the twilight's last gleaming?"

As the dawn grew lighter, Key saw the Stars and Stripes still flying above Fort McHenry. He finished his song. Someone added music. *The Star-Spangled Banner* is now our national anthem.

There are other songs we sing on the Fourth of July. A popular one in the North is the *Battle Hymn of the Republic.* It was written by Julia Ward Howe during the Civil War. She wrote it for the North.

But the song is sung to music written by a southerner named William Steffe.

In the South, *Dixie* is sung on the Fourth of July. This was the South's favorite song during the Civil War. Strangely enough, this song was written by a northerner, Daniel D. Emmett.

So on the Fourth of July the North sings a southern tune. And the South sings a song written by a northerner.

All together the whole nation sings:

"My country 'tis of thee
Sweet land of liberty
Of thee I sing."

This song was first sung in public on the Fourth of July. Some children sang it in a Boston church many years ago. *My Country 'tis of Thee* is sung to the same tune that the English use for their national anthem.

The two nations who fought in the Revolutionary War now share the same music.

4
Our National Symbols

Live American eagles used to be seen at Fourth of July celebrations. The great birds were very popular with the children.

The American eagle is the emblem of the United States. It is on the Great Seal of the United States too.

On the first Fourth of July, Congress decided that the new nation needed a seal. A seal is a stamp that goes on important papers.

You can see the Great Seal on the back of a dollar bill. The American eagle holds an olive branch in his right claw. The olive branch stands for peace.

In his left claw, the eagle holds thirteen arrows. There is one arrow for each of the thirteen original states. The arrows mean that the United States is ready to defend herself.

The eagle holds a ribbon in his beak. On the ribbon are some Latin words: *"E Pluribus Unum,"* or *"one out of many."* This means that the United States is one nation made out of many states.

There are few American eagles left today. If you are lucky, perhaps you will see one flying. The great bird is king of the sky.

Another national symbol is "Uncle Sam." You often see him on government posters.

And you see him in Fourth of July parades too. Uncle Sam is a make-believe person who stands for the United States.

During the War of 1812 there was a real man whose nickname was Uncle Sam. He worked at Troy, New York, for the United States government. He delivered packages for the army.

These packages were all marked with the letters "U.S." These stood for "United

States." They meant that the packages were United States property. Uncle Sam, the man who delivered them, had the same initials.

One day someone asked a man who was unloading packages, "What does U.S. stand for?"

The man scratched his head. Then he said, "Uncle Sam." He was joking.

The joke spread to the soldiers. They liked it. Soon Uncle Sam became a nickname for the United States.

In Fourth of July parades Uncle Sam is a tall man in a high hat. Part of the hat is striped red and white. And part is blue with white stars.

Uncle Sam's coat is blue with white stars too. His pants have red and white stripes. Uncle Sam certainly does look like an American flag.

5
A House Divided

On July 4, 1861, there was no celebration in the southern states. The South said it was no longer a part of the United States. The southerners would not celebrate a United States holiday.

The southern states wanted to build a new nation. They felt they had a right to leave the United States. But President Abraham Lincoln thought they were wrong.

"A house divided against itself," he had said, *"cannot stand."* Lincoln believed it was his duty to make the South stay a part of the United States.

One of the things that divided the people of the North and the South was Negro slavery. Many southerners wanted slavery. Most northerners were against it.

The North and the South fought a terrible war, the Civil War. Some people call it the War Between the States. At first, neither side seemed to be winning.

Two years later, on July 4, the North had something to celebrate. Its soldiers had just won the big battle of Gettysburg.

On the same day the northern army won still another major victory. Vicksburg, Mississippi, an important town in the South, surrendered. It was captured by General Ulysses S. Grant and his soldiers.

Grant got a letter from a friend. *"Glory, Hallelujah!"* the letter said. *"The best Fourth of July since 1776."*

All over the North there were big celebrations. People sang the *Battle Hymn of the Republic.*

In the South many people were sad. News of the defeat at Gettysburg was arriving by telegraph. Many southern soldiers had been killed.

The southern bands played *Dixie.* The people sang, *"In Dixie land I'll take my stand to live and die in Dixie."*

Two years later the war was over. The North had won. The Negro slaves were free. In the words of the Liberty Bell, liberty could now be proclaimed *"throughout all the land, unto ALL the inhabitants thereof."*

The freed slaves joined the celebration.

Now the great words *"all men are created equal"* would begin to have meaning for them.

In Charleston, South Carolina, a group of Negroes met in a church. A man read the Declaration of Independence to them. It was the first time they had heard it.

Many white southerners were glad the war was over too. Some of them started celebrating the Fourth of July again.

After all, the Declaration of Independence had been written by a southerner, Thomas Jefferson. George Washington, who also was a southerner, had made independence possible. He had led the American soldiers to victory over the English.

But there was no celebration in Vicksburg. It had been captured on the Fourth of July. Vicksburg did not celebrate the Fourth again for more than 80 years.

6
America's 100th Birthday

On July 4, 1876, America would be 100 years old. A hundredth birthday is called a centennial.

For several years America had been planning a great celebration. Independence had been declared in Philadelphia. So Philadelphia decided to have a world's fair during the summer of 1876.

Over in France a man named Frederic Bartholdi was working on the Statue of Liberty. He wanted it to be a birthday present from France to America.

He could not get the statue finished in time. But he did send the hand that holds the torch. It was set up on the fair grounds at Philadelphia.

In Ohio a man named Archibald M. Willard painted a picture. At first, he made a funny picture. It showed a Fourth of July parade in a little town.

Then he decided to change the painting. He would show a grandfather, a father and a grandson marching to battle in the Revolutionary War.

A 13-year-old boy posed for the drummer in the painting. His name was Henry Devereaux.

The picture was shown at the fair in Philadelphia. One day Henry Devereaux's mother took him to see it. People at the fair recognized him. He was pleased.

The picture became famous. At the

Philadelphia fair it was called *Yankee Doodle*. The picture is now called *The Spirit of '76*. Today the painting hangs in Marblehead, Massachusetts.

Another popular sight at the fair was a tame American eagle. He was named "Old Abe" after Abraham Lincoln. Old Abe had belonged to some Wisconsin soldiers during the Civil War. Many people at the fair bought his picture as a souvenir.

On the night of July 3, 1876, there were torchlight parades all over America. Just after midnight the nation would be 100 years old.

The biggest parade of all was held in Philadelphia. Flags flew from all the buildings. People jammed the sidewalks.

The sky was red with rockets as the great parade started toward Independence Hall. Drums beat. Trumpets blew. At exactly midnight the parade reached Independence Square.

A bell started ringing. It rang 13 times for the 13 original states.

When the bell stopped, a mighty shout went up from the crowd. Everyone sang *The Star-Spangled Banner.* Next they sang *"Praise God from whom all blessings flow."*

It was a fine beginning for America's 100th birthday party.

Early the next morning soldiers from the North and the South marched through the streets. It was the first time they had marched together since the Civil War.

When the Virginia soldiers passed Independence Hall, their band played *Dixie*. The northerners who lined the streets waved their handkerchiefs and cheered.

America was a united country again on its 100th Fourth of July.

7
The Liberty Bell

All the children who came to the Philadelphia fair wanted to see the Liberty Bell.

It could no longer ring. Many years before it had cracked. It was fixed. But while it was ringing to celebrate George Washington's birthday in 1846, it cracked again. This time it could not be repaired.

The Liberty Bell made many trips. Just before the English captured Philadelphia in 1777, the bell was taken to Allentown, Pennsylvania. It was hidden in the basement of a church. If the English had found the bell, they would have melted it to make bullets.

When the Americans returned to Philadelphia, the bell was brought back. It

rang to tell of the American victory at Yorktown. It rang on many other great days too.

After the Philadelphia fair, the bell went traveling again. People all over the country wanted to see it. It went to New Orleans, Chicago, Atlanta, Charleston, Boston and St. Louis.

The bell passed through many other cities and towns on a railroad car. School children lined the tracks to see it.

San Francisco asked Philadelphia to send the bell to a big fair there. At first, Philadelphia said no. The bell might be hurt on the long trip.

Soon a giant piece of paper came to Philadelphia. The paper was signed by 200,000 California children. They begged Philadelphia to send the bell. Finally the people in Philadelphia agreed.

Later, another giant piece of paper was sent to Philadelphia. It was signed by three and a half million children in the Midwest. The children wanted the bell to visit them.

The paper had nine miles of names! But people in Philadelphia said the bell was too old to make the trip.

The Liberty Bell does not travel anymore. But you can see it in Independence Hall in Philadelphia. Independence Hall is now a part of Independence National Historical Park. Children everywhere can see a picture of the Liberty Bell. It is on the back of many fifty cent pieces.

8

A Monument and Two Statues

Years ago, it became the custom to open new public buildings on the Fourth of July. And cornerstones are often laid on that day.

A cornerstone is a special stone put in place soon after work on a building has begun. The date is put on the outside. And interesting things are sealed up inside.

On July 4, 1848, a large crowd gathered in Washington, D. C. They had come to see the cornerstone laid for the Washington Monument. The monument would be in honor of the Revolutionary General and first President. Inside the cornerstone was a picture of Washington and a copy of the Declaration of Independence.

There were many important people at the ceremony.

There was also a 40-year-old American eagle! In 1824, this eagle had welcomed Lafayette on a visit to America. Lafayette was the Frenchman who had helped America win her independence.

It took a long time to finish the Washington Monument. Work stopped for many years because there was no money.

Finally the Washington Monument was opened to the public in 1888. It is 555 feet high. Today you can go to the top in a fast elevator. You can also climb the 898 steps.

Every Fourth of July, fireworks light the sky around the Washington Monument. Rockets burst around the top. Flaming rain falls to the ground. It is a grand sight.

Shortly before the Washington Monument was finished, America got a wonderful birthday present.

On July 4, 1884, France gave the Statue of Liberty to the United States. France had helped America win her liberty years before. The statue is a symbol of that liberty.

The Statue of Liberty is a woman. She holds a book in her left hand. Written on the book is *"July 4, 1776."*

In her right hand she holds a torch. Including the torch, she is 151 feet high. Her nose is four and a half feet long. And her mouth is three feet wide!

The statue was brought to America. At first there was not enough money to build a base for it to stand on.

School children all over America helped raise money. Sometimes they sent letters.

One letter read, "We have taken three lessons in French. We don't like it. But we love the good French people for giving

us the beautiful statue. We send you one dollar, the money we saved to go to the circus with."

Finally there was enough money. The statue was put up on Bedloe's Island in New York Harbor. Congress changed the island's name to Liberty Island in 1956.

American children wanted to give France a present too. They decided that their present should be a statue of Lafayette.

The children raised a lot of money. The government in Washington gave some money too.

On July 4, 1900, the statue was ready to be given to France. American flags flew all over Paris.

The statue had already been put up. But it was covered by a big American flag. The President of France came to receive the statue for his country.

Two boys stood ready to pull the flag from the statue. One of the boys was an American. The other was French. The French boy was the great-grandson of General Lafayette.

At a signal the boys uncovered the statue. There was General Lafayette carved out of stone. He was offering his sword to help America fight for her independence.

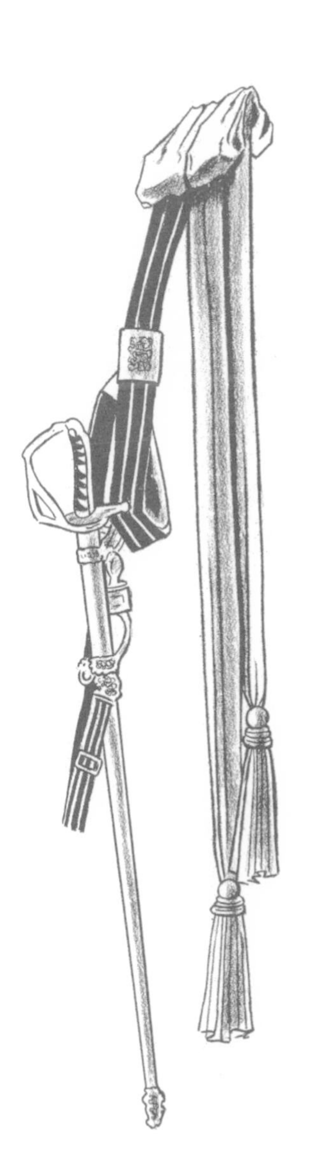

9

Fireworks

America got another great Fourth of July present in 1898. Spain and America were fighting the Spanish-American War.

On July 3, there was a big sea battle. The Spanish ships were led by Admiral Cervera. The American ships were led by Admiral William T. Sampson.

The American ships won the battle easily. That night Admiral Sampson sent a message to Washington. The message said, "*The fleet under my command offers the nation, as a Fourth of July present, the whole of Cervera's fleet.*"

The next day there were big celebrations all over the United States. It was one of the noisiest Fourths in the history of our country.

Fourth of July celebrations got even noisier in the next few years. Zip, bang, went the firecrackers! Many countries celebrated holidays with fireworks. But the Americans were celebrating too much. Many of the firecrackers were dangerous.

Every Fourth of July some children were killed by firecrackers. Many others had their fingers and hands blown off. Some had their eyes put out.

It looked as if more Americans were going to be killed celebrating independence than had been killed fighting for it.

Finally, some wise people tried to make Americans have a "Safe and Sane" Fourth. Towns passed laws against firecrackers.

In most places today only trained men are allowed to set off fireworks. Children watch from a safe distance. They see rockets climb into the sky and bombs burst in the air.

In 1918, the bombs and rockets were real. America was at war. She was helping England and France fight Germany. So many countries were fighting on each side that the war was called the World War.

Many American soldiers were in France. They were helping drive the Germans out.

"Lafayette, we are here," the Americans said. They meant they were paying

Lafayette back for his help in the American Revolution.

On July 4, 1918, an American in Paris put flowers on Lafayette's grave. Paris named a street after the American President, Woodrow Wilson.

Germany was defeated. There was peace, but not for long.

On July 4, 1942, America was fighting in World War II. She was fighting Germany, Italy and Japan. France, England and many other countries were on America's side.

On this July 4, fireworks were not allowed in American cities near the sea. The light they made might help enemy submarines sink American ships.

President Franklin D. Roosevelt spoke to the nation on the Fourth.

"We celebrate it this year, not in the

fireworks of make-believe, but in death-dealing reality of tanks and planes and guns and ships."

On July 4, 1945, the war was almost over. America and her friends were winning. So some of America's friends helped celebrate the Fourth of July.

An English battleship flew the American flag. This was the first time in history that an American flag had flown from a British battleship.

In England, cannon boomed 48 times in honor of the 48 American states. Long ago England and America had fought each other in the Revolutionary War. But now they were good friends.

10 Fifty Stars in the Flag

When America was young, the flag had 13 stars and 13 stripes. There was a stripe and a star for each state.

Congress decided to add a new star and stripe for each new state. Soon Vermont and Kentucky became states. The new flag had 15 stars and 15 stripes.

Many more states were being made. Congress was afraid the flag might get too big. So Congress made a new set of rules. After July 4, 1818, the flag would have only 13 stripes. These would stand for the 13 original states. No more stripes would be added.

Now a new star would be added for each new state. Flags with the new star would be flown for the first time on the Fourth of July. This would always be on the first Fourth after the new state was made.

On the fiftieth Fourth of July there were 24 states. So there were 24 stars in the flag. At the end of the Civil War there were 35 stars.

In 1912, Arizona became the 48th state. For almost fifty years the flag had only 48 stars. But on July 4, 1959, a new star was added. The new star was for Alaska.

The United States had bought Alaska from Russia in 1867. That year, Americans in Sitka, Alaska, were happy. They pulled down the Russian flag. The American flag took its place. This flag had 37 stars.

Alaska became a state in 1959. On July 4, the people in Sitka pretended that it was 1867 again. They flew a Russian flag. Then they pulled it down.

A new American flag was then run up on the flagpole. This flag had 49 stars. The 49th star was for Alaska.

The 49-star flag did not last long. On the very next Fourth of July another star was added. The new star was for Hawaii. Now there were 50 stars in the flag.

There was a big celebration in Hawaii. Airplanes raced across the sky.

At Fort McHenry in Maryland, there

U.S.

was a special celebration in Hawaii's honor. It was at Fort McHenry that Francis Scott Key wrote *The Star-Spangled Banner.*

Right after midnight on July 4, 1960, a new 50-star flag rose above the fort. Cannon boomed 50 times. The last boom was for Hawaii.

Rockets burst about the new flag. Thirty thousand people sang.

"And the rocket's red glare, the bombs bursting in air,
Gave proof through the night that our flag was still there.
Oh, say does that star-spangled banner yet wave
O'er the land of the free and the home of the brave?"